Blue Moon

Marilyn Halvorson

orca soundings

ORCA BOOK PUBLISHERS

National Library of Canada Cataloguing in Publication Data
Halvorson, Marilyn, 1948-

Blue moon / Marilyn Halvorson.

(Orca soundings)
First published: Don Mills, Ont.: Maxwell Macmillan Canada, 1994.
ISBN 1-55143-320-6

I. Title. II. Series.

PS8565.A462B68 2004   jC813'.54   C2004-900489-1

Summary: Can Bobby Jo take a beat-up old horse and turn her into champion barrel racer?

First published in the United States, 2004
Library of Congress Control Number 2004100596

Orca Book Publishers gratefully acknowledges the support for its publishing programs provided by the following agencies: the Government of Canada through the Book Publishing Industry Development Program (BPIDP), the Canada Council for the Arts, and the British Columbia Arts Council.

Cover design: Lynn O'Rourke
Cover photography: Getty Images

In Canada:
Orca Book Publishers
Box 5626 Stn B.
Victoria, BC Canada
V8R 6S4

In the United States:
Orca Book Publishers
PO Box 468
Custer, WA USA
98240-0468

Printed and bound in Canada
on New Leaf Eco, 100% post consumer waste paper

07 06 05 • 5 4 3 2

To Goldie,
I've owned a lot of good horses,
but only one great one. You were it.
—M.H.

Chapter One

"Sold!" the auctioneer yelled. "To the young redhead in the red jacket."

For a second I just sat there stunned. Out of the corner of my eye I could see a curl of hair above the shoulder of my jacket. The hair was red. The jacket was red. There was no getting out of it. I had just bought a horse.

But why had I bought this horse? I watched gloomily as the bony blue roan mare limped out of the sale ring. Her ears were laid back angrily. As the ring man swung the gate closed behind her, she lashed out and kicked it with both back hoofs. Oh, wow! Did I have a winner on my hands! How could I have been so stupid? What was my dad going to say? He lets me go to my first horse sale alone, on a school day even, and I mess up big-time. But sitting here wasn't going to help. Slowly I stood up and made my way down from the stands and toward the sales office.

I was partway through the barn area when a voice stopped me. It was a cool, lazy, laid-back voice. "Skippin' school, Bobbie Jo?"

I swung around and almost bumped into the guy who owned the voice. Cole McCall, the kid from the farm next to ours. Just who I needed to finish wrecking my day. I tossed my hair back. "That's an interesting question. Coming from the all-time champion at that sport," I said coldly.

I turned and kept on walking. Cole just laughed and fell into step beside me. I pretended he wasn't there.

"Where are you goin'?" he asked.

"To pay for my horse, if it's any of your business."

"You just bought a horse?" Cole's voice had taken on a new note of interest.

"That's what I said," I answered, looking straight ahead and walking a little faster. "Now why don't you go find some of your hoodlum friends and leave me alone?"

A look I couldn't quite get flickered across his face. For a second I almost thought there was a real person behind Cole McCall's grin. But then he gave a careless shrug. "Yeah, why not? The guys are better company than you. See ya around, Blue Jeans."

Cole had been calling me that ever since he first came into my grade ten class at West Valley High School last year. The nickname did fit my initials. It fit my clothes, too. But I still didn't want Cole McCall calling me that. I didn't want him calling me anything.

Maybe it was because I was afraid he kind of liked me. At least, my friend Julie said he did. But I wasn't about to get involved with a guy like Cole. He had a real attitude. He was always in trouble at school, mainly for skipping, and he didn't even try to come up with a good excuse for it. Besides, I wasn't about to go out with any guy who had longer hair than I did. I tossed my head and marched off to pay for the horse I shouldn't even have bought.

At the office I told the clerk my name and he flipped through some papers. "Okay, here it is. B.J. Brooks, lot number 79. All I need is a check for $690" His eyes widened as I dug in my pocket and came out with a fat roll of bills.

"Cash okay?" I asked. I'd emptied my piggy bank, dumped the jar of quarters I'd been saving since I was ten, and taken all the coins to the bank. Then I'd closed out my savings account and taken that in cash, too. It looked like a lot of money when I got it all in bills.

The clerk nodded. "Cash is fine. You're just the first person I've seen in a long time who actually has some."

I started counting out the money and thought about how much work I'd done to earn each one of those twenty-dollar bills. The profit from three years of raising 4-H calves, all those summers of cutting the neighbors' lawns. And I'd gathered up every cent and brought it here to buy this horse.

No, that wasn't true. I didn't bring it here to buy this horse. I came to buy a colt. A yearling at the oldest. A good, young quarter horse that I could train myself and make into a champion barrel horse. Buying a colt would mean it would be three or four years before I could actually race him. I hated waiting that long, but I didn't have a choice. If you watched your chance you could get a good colt for the money I had. A trained barrel horse, ready to go, would cost a few thousand.

So how had I set out to buy a colt with a future and wound up with a sour, beat-up, old mare that obviously had a past? I'd asked myself that question a lot of times in the last few minutes, but I still wasn't sure of the answer.

I should have realized from the start that the blue roan mare was a meat horse. If I hadn't known by the way she looked, I should have known by who was bidding on her. There were a couple of crafty old guys who always hung around the sales, picking up the horses that had hit the end of the trail. They bought for the meat packers and they were always on the lookout for a chance to buy cheap. Much as I hated the thought of any horse ending up that way, I knew it was a fact of life. I guess it was better than the horses being left to starve. Better than getting so old and crippled they got down and couldn't get up.

So why couldn't I have just left things alone and let nature take its course? Why did I have to go and buy this mare? It might have been her color that did it. When I was a little kid I had a picture book called *Lady, the Little Blue Mare*. It was about a blue roan horse and I read it until the cover fell off. Ever since, I'd wanted a horse that color more than anything else in the world. But blue roans are about as common as honest politicians. I guess I went a little crazy when I came across a blue roan I could actually own. Or maybe the real reason I bought her was because she was a rebel. I liked the way she held her head up. The way she fought back when she was pushed around.

While one half of my mind was thinking about that, the other half was counting out the money. "Six hundred, six hundred and twenty, six hundred and forty, six hundred and sixty, six hundred and eighty," I counted out loud. Suddenly I stopped. That was my last twenty I'd just tossed on the pile. I dug in my pocket for the other twenty I knew was there. Nothing but a well-worn Kleenex. I checked the other pocket. Empty as my kid sister's head. I checked the pockets of my jean jacket. Lint and two gum wrappers.

The clerk cleared his throat. "Another ten dollars, miss."

"I know, I know," I muttered, shooting him a dirty look. "Don't get your shirt in a knot. It's here somewhere." I made another panic-stricken tour of my pockets. That twenty dollars was not here anywhere. I could hear the people in the lineup behind me shuffling their feet.

"Miss," the clerk said firmly, "either you've got the money or you haven't. If you're short on cash, why don't you write a check for the last ten?"

"Because I don't have any money left in the bank," I muttered. "But I did have the cash. I know I did."

"Well," the clerk said wearily, "you don't now. Step aside and let these other people go ahead. I'll give you half an hour to come up with the cash or we'll have to resell the horse."

Resell the horse? Let him resell the horse and I'd be off the hook. I'd have my $690.00 and I wouldn't be stuck with that sorry excuse for an animal. I should have jumped right up and kissed that old clerk on his tobacco-stained mustache. But, oh no, not me. Right then and there I bristled up like a cornered cat and glared at him. "You will not resell that horse. I bought her fair and square and I'll get you your lousy ten bucks. You can count on it!"

Chapter Two

Okay, now, I told myself. This is not a problem. Just find somebody you know and ask them to lend you ten bucks. Half the farmers from West Valley are always at the auction market. One of our neighbors must be here.

Well, maybe not quite always. I made three tours through the whole auction market. Along the way I had the offer of a date—from an eighty-year-old guy with no teeth. I was yelled at twice for standing in front of somebody and blocking his view of the sale ring. And when I reached up to push my hair back at the wrong moment I almost bought another horse. But I didn't see a soul I knew.

I was getting desperate enough to call home and explain the mess I was in to my parents. I checked my watch and scrapped that idea. Right now, Mom would be at work driving the school bus and Dad would be out in the field planting green feed. But I had to think of something. The closer I got to losing that blue roan horse, the more I started to like her.

Then I caught a glimpse of Walt Devon. He was one of the meat buyers, running a string of sorry-looking old horses up the ramp into his trailer. When the last one was in, his helper closed the door behind it. "Ready to roll, boss?" he asked.

Devon picked a tidbit of leftover lunch out of a crack between his teeth. "Naw, don't get in a hurry, Bill. Think I might pick up another one cheap here in a minute."

That did it! Walt Devon was not going to haul my horse off to the packing plant. I took another desperate look around. Over by the corrals, three or four guys were throwing square bales onto a truck. I didn't recognize any of them at first. Then something about one of them caught my eye—long, curly blond hair, ragged denim jacket. Yeah, it was him all right. I never thought I'd be desperate enough to ask Cole McCall for the time of day, but I was stuck. I took a deep breath. "Cole?"

Either he didn't hear me or he pretended not to. He kept on tossing bales. Just talking to him was bad enough. Did I have to yell his name for all the world to hear?

"Cole!"

He set down a bale and slowly turned around. The two strangers he was working with turned to stare at me.

"Cole, I, uh, need to talk to you."

Cole gave me a cold look. "Don't bother me, Blue Jeans," he said between breaths. "We're busy." The other guys laughed. I could feel my face getting warm.

"Cole," I said through my teeth, "would you just come here, please?"

He gave his friends kind of a shrug. To me he gave a low bow and a taunting grin as he walked over. "What can I do for you, Blue Jeans?"

I held my temper. "Uh, Cole, do you have ten dollars?"

He gave me an unbelieving stare and then he laughed. "Do I look like I have ten dollars?"

I was in no position to be rude. I meant to be polite. Really, I did. But the words just came out. "No, you look like you should be standing in somebody's garden to scare the crows away. But I still need to know if you can lend me ten dollars."

That remark should have finished my chances of borrowing ten cents from Cole McCall. I couldn't believe it when he started to laugh. "You're somethin' else, Blue Jeans."

Before I could decide on an answer to that he reached into his pocket and came out with a crumpled five-dollar bill and some change. "That's all she wrote. Seven good enough?"

I shook my head. I couldn't come this close and give up. "Check your other pockets. Maybe you've got some more change."

He stared at me again for a minute, sighed and checked the other pocket of his jeans. He shook his head. "Out of luck, lady."

"Are you sure?"

Cole sighed. "Honest, Officer, I'm sure. You want to search me or what?"

I could feel my face warming up again. "No!" I blurted out. "But what about your jacket pockets?"

He shrugged and jammed his hands into the pockets of his ragged jean jacket. His right hand came out the bottom of the pocket. He laughed and waved it at me. I just glared at him. Then he brought out his left hand, closed.

"Well?" I demanded.

Slowly, he opened his hand. He was holding three matches, his truck keys—and four coins. I pounced on the money. A loonie, two quarters, two dimes and a nickel.

"Close enough! Give it to me quick." I held out my hand. "Please," I added, remembering to be polite this time.

"Uh-uh. Not until you tell me what you want it for."

I felt my temper fraying around the edges. If he kept this up the horse would be canned before I got back with the money. "To pay for the horse, okay?"

Cole raised his eyebrows. "Ten bucks for a horse? Must be a real winner." But he handed me the money.

"For your information, I paid 690 dollars for her. I'm just short ten dollars. I'll pay you back at school tomorrow—if you happen to show up."

"Wouldn't miss it, Blue Jeans," he said, starting to turn away. "I better get back to work before I get fired."

"You work here?"

"Yeah, I work here. You think throwing those bales around is a hobby? Low-rent bodybuilding or something?"

I glanced at the muscles in his forearms below his rolled-up sleeves. Throwing bales wasn't doing Cole any harm in the body-building department.

"Hey, kid!" one of the guys over at the truck called. "Get over here. You can talk to your girlfriend on your own time."

Cole looked at me. "Now look what you've gone and done to my reputation," he said with a taunting grin. He turned and was gone before I could say thanks—if I'd been going to say thanks, that is.

Chapter Three

I recounted my $680 and pushed it across to the clerk. Then I handed over Cole's bills and change. Last, I gave him a smoothed-out gum wrapper. He looked down at the money, flicked the gum wrapper aside and then looked up at me. "Short a buck and a quarter," he growled.

"I know that," I said. "That's why I gave you this." I pushed the gum wrapper back across the desk.

"I don't want a gum wrapper."

"Read it. Never mind. Maybe you can't. I'll read it to you. 'IOU a dollar twenty-five. Signed, B.J. Brooks.' I'll mail you the money tomorrow."

The clerk sighed wearily and rubbed his head as if he had a real bad headache.

"Aw, come on!" I burst out. "I swear you'll get the money. You aren't gonna re-sell my horse on account of a buck and a quarter, are you?"

The clerk didn't answer. He just reached into his pocket and brought out a handful of change. He picked out a loonie and a quarter and put them on top of my pile of money. Then he took the bill of sale and scrawled PAID IN FULL across it in big, black letters. He handed it to me.

"Hey, uh, thanks,'" I said. "That was nice of you."

"Just do me a favor, miss. Take your horse and go. Go far and go fast."

I took the bill of sale and went. I had to get my horse and load her into Dad's stock trailer. The thought of hauling her home made me more nervous than I wanted to admit. I hadn't done much driving with the trailer behind me. And what if I couldn't get the horse into the trailer? Stop worrying about that, I told myself. After all, she hadn't walked from wherever she came from. Somebody must have loaded her.

I glanced down the row of parked trailers. A kid about my age was leading a big, strong-looking red mare up to the back of a trailer. I remembered seeing that horse sell. The meat buyers had been the only ones bidding on her, too. I guessed it was because of her age. She was a real old horse. But at the last minute this kid had jumped in and bought her. I wondered at the time if he knew what he was doing. Now I watched as he opened the trailer door and stepped inside without even looking back. The big mare lifted her feet neatly and calmly stepped into the trailer, too. The boy came out, fastened the door and got into the truck. Loading his horse had taken about two minutes. Maybe the kid did know what he was doing. At least the old mare had manners.

Okay, B.J., you saw how that guy did it. Walk right in and assume the horse is going to follow. Don't look back. Never let her know you're not sure of yourself.

I led the horse to the trailer and stepped right up into it as smoothly as I could—considering the tightness of my jeans. I took two more steps inside the trailer. The rope went taut so suddenly that I almost did the world's first sideways bungee jump. I decided that now might be a good time to look back. My roan mare had stopped dead at the trailer door. She was standing there rooted to the ground like a big oak tree, and I could see she had no plans for travel.

Must be time for Plan B. Now, what was Plan B? Well, there was always the oats. My old pony would walk through fire for oats. I got out the pail I'd brought along, scooped out a handful and held them out to the roan. Her eyes lit up with interest. From the way her ribs showed through her moth-eaten hair, I'd bet she hadn't seen a whole lot of oats lately. She stuck her lips out, gathered up a few kernels and crunched them thoughtfully. "Good girl," I said. Then I backed a step closer to the trailer, taking up the slack of the rope. My horse blew suspiciously through her nostrils and took a step back. Then she just stood there, eyeing me like she knew I was up to something. She refused to even sniff the next handful of oats I held out. This was one horse with self-control.

Plan C. Get tough. I led the mare around in a circle and up to the trailer again. Again she balked at the door. "Come here!" I commanded, sounding tough, I hoped. The horse didn't move. I gave the rope a little jerk. The mare threw up her head and gave the rope a bigger jerk. "Come on, horse," I said through my teeth. I gave the rope a good yank. The mare reared, lunged backward and almost fell on her back. The rope went sizzling through my right hand. I managed to grab on with the other hand just in time to keep her from getting away. She came down on all four feet, got her balance back and stood there snorting and trembling.

I looked at the palm of my right hand. The rope had burned most of the top few layers of skin off. The burn was bright pink and oozing clear liquid. That was going to really hurt in a few minutes. As a matter of fact, it hurt enough already.

I sank down on the edge of the trailer floor and sat blowing cool air on my hand and staring out at my horse. She glared back at me from the far end of the rope, waiting for my next move. Unfortunately, I didn't have a next move. In fact, if I'd been the crying type this would have been a real good time to start blubbering. But I didn't. I just sat there with my head in my hands and tried to think.

"Anything I can do, Blue Jeans?" My head shot up so fast I spooked the horse, and she jumped back, almost giving me another rope burn. "I was watchin' you try to load her from the hay truck over there," Cole said. He was looking down at me with kind of a half-grin on his face. "Didn't look like you were havin' much luck."

This was all I needed. Cole McCall rubbing in the fact that I'd bought an outlaw. About five nasty comments ran through my head. But, for once, none of them made it out of my mouth. "You got that right," was all I said.

"I know a trick that sometimes works when a horse won't load any other way. Want me to give it a try?"

I shrugged. "You want to play cowboy hero, go ahead."

Cole just smiled and uncoiled the rope he'd brought along. He tied one end to a steel brace on the side of the trailer. Then he walked around the mare, bringing the other end of the rope with him but leaving lots of slack.

"Okay," he said, "you try to lead her in and I'll bring the rope around tight behind her rump. Sometimes a horse steps forward when they feel the push from behind."

"Yeah?" I said doubtfully. "And sometimes the horse just kicks the teeth out of whoever's back there."

Cole grinned. "Yeah, that too. But that's not your problem. You just worry about getting out of the way if she comes in with a flyin' leap."

"Yeah, right," I said, my voice tired. "And the man in the moon had better be ready to get out of the way if she takes a flyin' leap up there, too."

Cole ignored that. "Okay," he said. "Try and get her to come forward."

I gave a pull on the halter rope. The mare showed the whites of her eyes and started to step backward. Cole pulled on the rope so it snugged up around her hindquarters. She gave a startled snort and flicked her ears back to check out what was happening. I could see her getting ready to freak out. "Give her another pull," Cole ordered. I did.

The mare reared. Cole took in the slack and pulled the rope up tighter behind her. I had a hunch the mare was going to rear again. If she did, she'd bash her head against the top of the door frame. Then I felt the tension in the rope change. I saw the mare gather her muscles. The next thing I knew she'd taken a flying leap up into the trailer. It was more reflexes than brains that made me take a flying leap off to the side before she landed on top of me. Then the trailer door slammed behind the horse. She was blowing through her nostrils with a kind of terrified snort.

I did the only thing I could think of. I reached out a hand, touched a quivering, sweating shoulder and said, "Easy, girl, you're all right." I'm sure my shaking voice didn't come out real easy, but the horse stopped snorting.

Just then the trailer's side door opened and Cole looked in. "Aren't you coming out, Blue Jeans?" he asked innocently.

I gave him a fierce glare as I climbed out the door. "Thanks a lot for locking me in there with her," I said.

Cole shrugged. "You didn't want her to get out again, did you?" He slid the latch into place and breathed a big sigh. "Okay,

Blue Jeans, you got yourself a horse in a trailer. Try not to spill her on the way home, okay?"

I flashed him a look. "After all that, I'm—"

A voice interrupted me. It was Merv Miller, one of the owners of the auction barn. He was staring at Cole. "This is the second time today you've been talking when you're supposed to be working. Last Thursday you didn't bother showing up at all. I've had it with you, McCall."

"Hey, come on, Mr. Miller," Cole said. "I explained all that. And I was just helping out—"

"Save it for somebody who cares, McCall. I don't. And don't bother showing up for work next week. I'll mail your wages."

Cole gave him an unbelieving stare. "You're firing me?"

"You catch on quick, kid." He started to walk away but Cole grabbed his arm.

"Come on, Mr. Miller, you can't do that. I need this job."

Miller shook off his hand and gave him an icy stare. "I just did. Touch me again and I'll have you up for assault." He turned and strode off.

Cole swore under his breath and slammed his fist into the back of the trailer so hard it spooked the mare. She slammed a hoof against the gate.

"Cole, I..." I began, but Cole spun around and just kept walking away.

Chapter Four

I drove home carefully, like I was hauling a load of dynamite—which in a way I probably was. And all the way home I kept on thinking about Cole McCall. About him getting fired, I mean. And how it was my fault. And that really made me mad because it wasn't my fault. Did I ask him to come over and stick his nose into my business while he was supposed to be working? No, it wasn't my fault. But I still couldn't stop feeling guilty about it.

At last I was home. I wheeled the truck up our lane, cut the engine and for a minute just sat there letting the tension ease out of my muscles. But then the kitchen door opened and the welcoming committee came pouring out. Mom, Dad and my stupid twelve-year-old sister. I took a deep breath and got out of the truck.

"Thank goodness you're home. We were beginning to think you'd had an accident." Mom, always the worrier.

"So what'd you buy? Bet it's not any good." Sara, my upbeat sister.

"Hmm, no major body damage," Dad said with a grin as he pretended to check out the truck and trailer. "Well, open the door, Bobbie Jo. Let's see the colt that's going to be a future barrel racing champion."

I hadn't been looking forward to this moment. "Well, it's not exactly a..." I began, but Dad was already opening the trailer door. I just had time to catch the halter rope before the mare exploded out of there like a blue tornado. Before I got her under control she managed to drag the rope through my already rope-burned hand. "Whoa!" I roared furiously and, amazingly, she stopped. She stood there trembling and eyeing my family like they'd just landed from Mars. They stood there looking at her in about the same way.

"Well, she's, uh, an interesting color," my mother managed at last.

Dad looked her up and down and I could see he was trying hard to say the right thing. "A little good feed might make quite a difference" was the best he could come up with.

Sara stepped up and inspected the horse at close range. "Bobbie Jo, that is the most totally gross excuse for a horse I ever saw in my life."

The mare swung her head around and took a nip at Sara's leg. It was the first intelligent thing I'd seen her do. Unfortunately, she missed.

Dad cleared his throat. "Well, I don't know about anybody else, but I'm starved. Put your horse in the corral, Bobbie Jo, and let's go get some supper."

I led the mare over to the corral where my old pony, Patchy Pete, was standing. Patchy had his head over the fence, waiting to meet his new friend. I shooed him out of the way and led the mare inside. Patchy rushed over like a Welcome Wagon hostess about to greet the new neighbor. The mare took one sniff at him, whirled around and landed both hind hoofs on his well-padded side. Patchy scuttled over to cower in the far corner of the corral. He looked downright disappointed—just like the rest of the family.

Fortunately, we had to rush through supper so no one had time to talk much. Sara had ballet lessons—yeah, I have a sister who actually takes ballet lessons—and Mom had to drive her to town by seven. That meant Dad and I got stuck with the dishes, but it was worth it just to get Sara out of my sight.

I was up to my elbows in greasy water when Sara passed by on her way out of the house. "Have a nice time with your moth-eaten horse," she said sweetly. "Oh, and your twenty dollars is on your dresser."

"My what?" I dropped the frying pan I was washing and slopped a tidal wave of soapy water onto the floor.

"Well, you don't have to take a hairy over it. You had a whole pile of them lying there this morning while you were in the shower. Mom forgot to give me money to get my hair cut and she was already gone, so I just borrowed a twenty from you. It's not as if I stole it or something. I gave it back. You probably didn't even miss it..."

I couldn't say a word. There are times when words just can't say how you feel like a greasy dishrag can. I was out of that sink and had Sara cornered and half the freckles scrubbed off her face before Dad yelled at me to leave her alone. I got a big lecture from him on mature behavior after Mom and Sara left. But the revenge had been well worth it. Besides, I caught Dad grinning a little when he was supposed to be glaring. He's probably the only person on earth who even comes close to understanding me.

Later, as I sat sort of studying for my last exam of the year, Dad was going through the mail. Out loud. "Bill, bill, bill," he muttered, tossing the first three envelopes in a pile. He paused a minute, studying a folder the government had sent out. "Student Farm Employment Program. Hey, maybe they'll actually pay you for helping me on the farm all summer."

"What?" I came to full attention.

He read on for another few seconds. "Oh, forget it, Bobbie Jo. Fine print says the government will pay half the wages if a farmer hires a student for the summer. But the student can't be a member of your own family."

"What a rip-off," I muttered. I'd gone from poor to rich to poor again in one split second.

"Well, so much for that," Dad said. "I don't know of any other kids who'd want to spend their summer stacking bales and hauling manure." He flicked the folder toward the garbage. And with a move that would have made any big-league shortstop proud, I picked it off in mid-flight. Dad raised his eyebrows questioningly.

"I think you could be wrong about that, Dad," I said slowly. "What if I can find someone who wants the job?"

Dad scratched his head. "Well now, that depends. Is this mysterious person going to be worth as much to have around as you are?"

"Not even close," I said with a grin. "But I think he really needs the work. Is it a deal?"

Dad shrugged. "Sure, I'll give it a shot." Then he got a teasing look in his eye. "This guy must be someone pretty special for you to go to all this trouble."

"Not exactly," I told him. "It's just because of a little debt I owe."

Cole did actually show up for school the next day, but he was in no mood for a visit. First

I tried to give him the money I owed him. He just shook his head and turned away.

"Come on, Cole, take it. I said I was gonna give it back and I meant it."

He shot me a smoldering look over his shoulder. "Forget it, Blue Jeans. Eight bucks ain't gonna make a whole lot of difference now." He started to walk away.

I followed. "What is it with you anyhow? I didn't ask you to help me load the horse. You don't need to blame me for what happened."

"Who said I was blamin' you?" he said, still walking.

"It's pretty obvious you are. Anyway, that's sort of what I need to talk to you about. A job, I mean."

That stopped him in his tracks. "What job?"

"I know where you can get a summer job. If you want another job, that is."

"Want?" Cole said with a bitter laugh. "Want don't have nothing to do with it. Need is more like it. So where's this job?"

"At my place. Helping my dad with haying and stuff."

"Oh, I get it. You got to feelin' a little guilty so you talked your old man into inventing a job for the poor boy, huh?" He started walking again. "Well, you can forget it, Blue Jeans. I don't need your charity."

I caught up to him again. "Look, Cole McCall, I couldn't care less if you take this job or not, but one thing you better know. It's not charity. And the job's not invented. There's plenty of work on our farm to keep a dozen guys like you busy. The only reason I'm not getting this job myself is that the government won't help pay for family. Job starts at eight o'clock tomorrow morning. If you had a little less pride and a little more ambition you might show up. But I won't hold my breath waiting for you." I spun around and stalked away, wondering why I'd even bothered to try.

All through my chemistry exam, Cole kept interrupting my thoughts. Here I'd gone and knocked myself out to get him another job and he decides it's time to get an attitude. Well, that was fine with me. I didn't want him hanging around all summer anyway. But I still had trouble keeping my mind on chemistry.

My last exam—and the school year—finally ended. I bounded off the bus, ready to get to know my new blue horse. I climbed up on top of the corral rail and just sat there studying her for a while, mentally checking off her good and bad points. The list of bad points grew a lot faster than the one of good points. Number one: She was so skinny her ribs stuck out. Okay, at least I could fix that. Lots of grass and some oats would do the trick. Number two: She limped on her left front leg. I hoped it was something she was going to get over real quick. Number three: She was all scarred up in half a dozen places. Some of the scars looked like teeth marks from other horses. If she treated all horses the way she'd treated Patchy last night, I could see how she wouldn't be real popular in the corral.

She also had a cinch sore behind her front leg. It was nearly healed so it wasn't going to be a problem. And it did prove one thing. If someone had ridden her enough to leave her cinch sore, she must at least be broke to ride. I decided I could move that point to the good side. There were a few more things I could have mentioned on the bad side—her mean temper for one—but I decided to move on to the good stuff.

Her color. That was her best point. How do you describe a blue roan? Well, believe it or not, they really are kind of blue. Not sky blue. Kind of smoky gray-blue. It comes from a blend of gray and black and white hairs all mixed together. That color covers the main part of the blue roan's body. The mane, tail, legs and head are usually jet black. Put it all together and it's about the neatest outfit a horse could wear. Sort of like they're all dressed up for dinner at a fancy restaurant.

I decided it was about time for the moment of truth. The moment when I found out what happened when I actually got on this outlaw. I couldn't actually ride her anywhere till her limp got better, but it wouldn't hurt to get on her. At least, it wouldn't hurt her. What happened to me remained to be seen. I went to the barn and got a halter. Coming back out I met Dad.

"Hey, B.J., I've been looking for you. Got time to help me out for an hour or two?" I sighed inside but gave my dad a grin. He never asks for help unless he really needs it.

"Sure, Dad. What's happening?"

"I'm going to see if I can get that last little field of green feed planted. I think it's finally dried up enough not to get stuck on it. Can you drive me out in the truck and help me fill the seed drill with oats?"

"No problem."

I gave the roan mare one last glance over my shoulder. I really had wanted to get on her today. She gave me a look that showed quite a lot of the whites of her eyes. I don't think she really wanted anybody to get on her.

By the time I got done helping Dad, it was starting to get dark. My first try at riding this horse wasn't something to rush into with ten minutes of daylight left. She'd still be there tomorrow, I hoped.

Then another thought hit me. Keeping her and Patchy in the corral eating hay was kind of a waste. Patchy always grazed out in the pasture with the milk cows. Now that the mare had been here for a day and was used to Patchy's company, I didn't figure she was likely to try to jump out.

"See, you blue streak of misery," I said, opening the gate. "I trust you. I'm giving you your freedom."

Patchy marched calmly out the gate and instantly attacked a patch of grass. The roan eyed me suspiciously. She made a slow approach to the opening, hugged the side farthest from me and eased her way out, pretending to be invisible. At last she was past me. Then she ducked her head, kicked up her heels, gave a defiant squeal and lit out across the pasture. I just shook my head. Well, at least she wasn't all that lame.

Chapter Five

The first day of summer vacation. No bus to catch. No last-minute homework to finish. No fighting Sara for just five minutes out of her long-term lease on the bathroom. I was going to sleep and sleep and sleep...

"Bobbie Jo! Get out here right now." It was Dad's voice and he sounded like he meant business. I unglued my eyelids and stared at the figures on the clock radio.

Seven-fifteen. Seven-fifteen on the first day of the holidays? Give me a break, Dad. "Bobbie Jo!" The volume was rising.

I muttered something that started in my brain as "I'm coming," but came out of my mouth more like "Mmph hmhm." I managed to get my sweatshirt on backwards. Then it took three tries before I stopped trying to fit both my legs into one leg of my jeans. Finally, I staggered to the kitchen.

Dad was the only one up. He usually got up first to get the cows in the barn and fed their grain. Either Mom or I went out a little later to help with the milking. Princess Sara did not involve herself with cows. They smelled.

"What's wrong?" I asked.

Dad pointed out the kitchen window. "Take a look out there and you'll see what's wrong. That crazy new horse of yours."

I looked out the window expecting to see that the roan had jumped the fence and was grazing in the pea patch or something. But she was right there in the cow pasture where I'd left her. The only problem was that she had all thirty of Dad's prize Holstein cows cornered in the far end of the pasture. She was standing in front of the herd like a prison guard or something. As I watched. one of them made a halfhearted attempt to start toward the barn. Instantly, the mare flattened her ears and made a dive in the cow's direction. The cow made an ungraceful retreat back into the bunch.

I couldn't believe my eyes. What did the mare think she was doing? In all Patchy's years of grazing with the cows, the worst thing he'd done was steal the juiciest clump of clover from some slow-witted cow. Now I'd gone and got a horse who thought she was a cowgirl.

Dad's voice interrupted my thoughts. "You've got exactly two minutes to get that horse out of..."

I tore out of the house and the slamming of the kitchen door cut off the end of his sentence. I grabbed a halter out of the barn and raced across the pasture. Racing up to any horse you plan to catch is not exactly brilliant. Racing up to this horse sent her galloping to the opposite end of the pasture. It didn't get me one bit closer to catching her, but at least the milk cows escaped. They went streaming gratefully off to the barn for the morning milking.

I got the roan mare cornered. She and I looked at each other. "Whoa," I growled between my gritted teeth. The mare stood still, trembling a little. I took another step toward her. "Whoa," I said again. As I reached out to slip the halter rope around her neck, she swung around on her hind legs and took off across the pasture again. As she went she gave a light little whinny. It sounded an awful lot like a laugh to me.

I wasn't laughing. I was sweating and puffing and saying unladylike things under my breath. Dad told me once when I was little that to catch a horse you had to be smarter than the horse. That didn't say a lot for my IQ. I charged across the pasture, trying to cut her off at the pass. Suddenly my foot hit something slippery and shot out from under me. Next thing I knew, I had landed on the seat of my pants in a pile of very fresh, very wet and very smelly cow manure. Slowly, I picked myself up, wiped off the thickest of the stinking mess and then washed my hands off on the dew-wet grass. I kept thinking that if I had just minded my own business, that blue roan mare might be in a can by now.

I set my teeth and started after her again. She was standing in the corner by the barn. By now I'd lost all idea of the smart way to catch her. I just plodded straight toward her. She didn't move. I knew she was waiting until the last second for a flashy getaway. I kept plodding. She kept standing. I was within reaching range. Slowly, my hand went out. She didn't move as I slipped the halter over her head and fastened the buckle. That's when I took my first breath in quite a while. I had her.

I stood glaring at her. No horse had ever put me through anything like that before.

She deserved...What did she deserve? A good beating? Or maybe she'd had a few too many good beatings. Maybe that was why she wasn't about to trust anybody. But one thing was for sure, abusing a hard-to-catch horse wasn't going to make her any easier to catch next time.

"Atta girl," I whispered, swallowing my fury. "See, nothin' bad happens to you when you get caught." I turned to run a soothing hand along her neck. As I did, something caught my eye. A beat-up old black truck parked halfway down the lane. Cole McCall's truck. And the great Cole McCall himself was sitting on the hood watching me. He looked like he was taking in the wild-horse race at the Calgary Stampede. And he was laughing.

Chapter Six

For a minute I was too stunned to do anything but stare at him as he strolled over to the fence. By the time he got to me, I wasn't stunned any longer. I was furious. "What do you think you're doing here?" I blurted out.

He checked his watch. "Working. In about ten minutes, if the job starts at eight like you said it did."

"Job?" I echoed. "You said you didn't want the job."

He shook his head. "Wrong again, Blue Jeans. I said I didn't like your reasons for offering it. I didn't say I wouldn't take it." He gave me a strange look and sniffed the air. "Interesting perfume you're wearing. What's it called? Cow Pasture Memories?"

I felt my face do an instant replay of the recent sunrise. "Cole, if you don't get out of my sight in the next..." But before I could finish he bent over and ran his hand down the mare's left front leg, the one she limped on. The mare laid back her ears and I could see she was getting ready to take a bite out of his backside—and I was going to cheer when she did. But Cole read her mind and straightened up in time to catch her with her teeth bared and nowhere to bite. He gave her a slap on the neck. "Knock it off, horse. You've got a worse disposition than your owner. Part owner, that is. How much did we pay again, Blue Jeans?"

I glared at him. "I paid $680 and you're taking your lousy $8.75 back."

He shook his head. "Uh-uh. I think we could've done worse. I'm stayin'" He started back toward his truck. "That's just a strained muscle in her leg. She'll heal up pretty fast."

Oh, right, now Mr. Know-It-All was a horse doctor, too. I ignored him and started for the corral with the horse. Halfway there his voice stopped me again. "Hey, Blue Jeans, aren't you supposed to wear the picture on the front of your shirt?"

I soon found out that having Cole working for Dad didn't mean that I was going to spend the summer polishing my nails. Dad found plenty of work for both of us. Actually, I was glad he did.

I'd spent seventeen years being Dad's right-hand man. I wasn't going to quit just because there was a guy around.

Right after supper was the first chance I got to spend some time working with the mare. As soon as we finished eating,

I excused myself and headed outside. To tell the truth, I couldn't get out of there fast enough. Good old Mom had decided that since Cole was working here right up until suppertime, he could just as well eat with us. Two meals a day across the table from that mocking grin was enough to spoil even my appetite.

I caught the mare easily enough in the corral and tied her up. Then I got my saddle and blanket. "Easy girl," I soothed, letting her sniff the blanket and then laying it on her back. Then the saddle. No reaction. Not even when I pulled the cinch up tight. I led her around a little. Okay, there was only one thing left to do. Get on her and find out what she planned to do about it.

I lined her up facing into a corner. If she did decide to explode, I might at least have a chance to get settled in the saddle first. "Whoa now, roan. Be nice, okay?" I took the reins in my left hand and got a firm grip on the saddle horn with my right. Then I started to put my foot in the stirrup. That's when I caught a glimpse of something over my shoulder. I brought my foot back to earth and spun around. "You work here, Cole. You don't live here," I said, giving him a nasty look. "You can go home now."

He just grinned and stepped up a rail higher on the corral fence. "I'll get there, Blue Jeans. Just wanted to see how our horse was coming along. Go ahead and get on. Unless havin' me here distracts you too much."

I rolled my eyes. "You couldn't distract me if you ran through the pasture in your underwear throwing away hundred-dollar bills. But if you're gonna hang around, at least shut up so you don't distract the horse."

"My lips are sealed." He climbed up on the top rail and made himself comfortable.

I sighed and turned back to the horse. I tried to recapture the confidence I'd worked up a few minutes before but to tell you the truth, I was distracted as all get-out.

I gathered the reins and my wits. Then I stuck my foot in the stirrup and swung aboard, making sure to land lightly. There was a long period of silence in which the horse tried to decide what to do about me. "Easy girl, I'm not gonna hurt you." Whether she was planning to hurt me was probably a lot more to the point. The mare wiggled her ears a little. Nothing else happened.

It finally occurred to me that I couldn't just sit there on the horse forever. Especially with Cole sitting there watching me with that irritating little grin on his face. Okay, here goes nothing, I thought. I nudged the mare's sides with my heels—and waited for her to erupt like a volcano.

She moved forward at an easy walk. One trip around the corral and I remembered to start breathing again. Two trips around the corral and I loosened my deathgrip on the reins. Three trips and the mare started tossing her head restlessly. I knew what her problem was. All horses hate being ridden around and around in tight circles.

I glanced over at Cole. "If you're gonna hang around, you could at least open the gate so I can take her out in the pasture," I said.

Cole lazily unfolded himself from his perch on the corral fence. "So you think you can handle her out there, huh?" he asked.

"Get real, McCall. This horse hasn't even twitched. What do you think, I'm scared of her or something?"

Cole shrugged and wandered over to open the gate. The mare moved smoothly out. We made a tour of the pasture. Halfway around, I gave her a little squeeze with my knees and she broke into a trot. I could feel her favoring her bad leg when she trotted so I turned her back toward home.

Near the fence she suddenly gave her head a little duck. In the next instant, her hind hoofs were kicking at the sky. The move surprised me so much it was a miracle I didn't sail over her head and do a one-point landing on my nose. But I stayed with her and followed my instincts—which were to pull her head up and give her a good kick in the ribs. "Knock it off!" I yelled, too mad to think about what she might do next. What she did was collect herself neatly and fall back into a ladylike trot. One ear cocked back at me and she turned her head enough to glance at me with one calm, dark eye. Just testing, I think she would have said.

I rode her back to where Cole was waiting and got off. "She's gonna be just fine," I said. "All she needs is a little time for her leg to heal and then she'll be ready to start on barrels."

Cole grinned. "Yeah, either that or saddle bronc."

"You mean that little crow hop? I hardly even noticed it. You didn't think she was gonna dump me, did you?"

He gave me a wicked grin. "Well, for a second there I did have hopes. But I guess I must have imagined that big patch of daylight between you and the saddle, huh?"

"Get your eyes checked, Cole." I started to lead the mare away.

"Hey," he said. "Hang on a minute."

"Now what?"

"Just lookin' at this brand," he said, running his hand along her shoulder. "Never seen it before. Wonder where she came from."

"The bill of sale said some outfit called Wagon Wheel Ranches. I figured that's what the brand was supposed to be—even if the spokes don't line up very even."

"Sure is a sloppy job. But what can you expect from somebody who keeps their horses in this kind of shape?" He gave the mare's thin, scarred-up body one more look and shook his head. Then he checked his watch. "Hey, I didn't know it was this late. I gotta get home."

"No kidding? So soon?" I said with a sigh of relief.

Cole just laughed at me. "See you in the morning, Blue Jeans."

"Not if I see you first," I muttered as he jumped into his old truck and took off in a spray of dust and gravel.

Chapter Seven

Mom and I were just finishing breakfast the next morning when the phone rang. Mom picked it up. "Hello? Oh, yes, hi, Cole."

Cole? Now what? Maybe one day of exciting life on a dairy farm had been enough for him. Maybe he wasn't coming back. That thought should have made my day. I wondered why it didn't.

Mom was talking again. "No, he's already gone out to milk. Can I take a message for him?" She listened a minute. "Oh, I'm sure that will be okay. Half an hour won't matter that much. All right. Bye." She hung up.

I was going to ask what that was all about when Sara stumbled into the kitchen, still in her pajamas. "Was that for me?" she asked through a yawn.

I jumped at the chance to rattle her chain a little. "No, Princess, it was not for you. Who do you know that gets up before noon?"

She stuck her nose in the air. "Well, at least I have friends who call me. I don't spend my life looking at, talking to and smelling like a horse. You never have time for people." Then, with a sly grin, she added, "Except for Cole baby, that is. Are you actually going out with him?"

"You shut up about me and Cole. I wouldn't go out with him if he was the last..." Before I had the words out I was halfway out of my chair and getting ready to wring her scrawny neck. But my mother's strong hand landed on my shoulder and plopped me back in my chair.

"Stop it, both of you. There are two months of holidays ahead and there is no way I plan to spend that time as a referee. Get along or, so help me, I'll have the two of you washing every wall in this house with a toothbrush."

My mother can and will make good on that kind of a threat. Sara and I sat glaring at each other until Mom broke the silence. "Speaking of Cole, that was him on the phone. He's going to be a little late for work because he has to drive his dad somewhere. Strange," she added thoughtfully, "I always thought his mother was a single parent. She waits tables at the Sunshine Cafe, I've seen her around town a few times and met her on the road. But she's never had a man with her."

Sara narrowed her eyes. "I bet his dad's an escaped convict and he has to stay home so nobody sees him. Maybe Cole's gotta take him to meet his partners so they can do another bank job."

Mom groaned and rubbed her forehead like she might have a headache already. "Spare us, Sara. Since you're up, hurry and eat and then go ahead and clean up the kitchen. It's time I was out helping your dad."

"Yeah, me too," I muttered. The faster we dropped the subject of Cole McCall and his family, the better I'd like it. Still, all the way to the barn I wondered just what was going on. If Cole's dad needed to go somewhere, why didn't he just drive himself? And why didn't anybody ever see this Mr. McCall around? Maybe he was a hopeless drunk who just sat home drinking up the grocery money and couldn't drive because he'd lost his license. Maybe he was mean and violent and beat Cole and his mom. Maybe that was why Cole hung around here half the night—because he was scared to go home. I was so busy thinking crazy maybes that I almost walked into a fence post.

Cole came to work before eight-thirty, apologized to Dad for being late and mainly ignored me. He didn't have any more to say to Dad than what it took to be polite, either. Before I had time to wonder about that, Dad announced what we were going to do. First we had to tear out a big section of old barbed wire fence. Then we'd cut out all the willows that had grown up and tangled in the wire, and put in all new posts. Real fun. So much fun that I almost decided to skip working with the horse and just collapse for the evening instead. But I didn't. Now that I knew the mare was actually going to let me ride her, I wanted to find out more about her.

As soon as I'd shoveled in the last spoonful of dessert, I excused myself and headed for the corral. With the mood Cole had been in all day, I thought I wouldn't have to bother with him hanging around me. Wrong again. I'd no sooner got the mare saddled up than there he was, leaning on the fence and watching me.

I got on the mare with more confidence this time. She sensed it, too. I could feel a calmness in her muscles. I rode her twice around the little corral. Then I looked at Cole and nodded toward the gate. He bowed like a well-behaved slave and opened it. I trotted the mare around the pasture. The lameness was still there, but a little less than yesterday, I thought.

Then I nudged her into a lope. I felt her muscles tense and saw her head start to go down. "Oh, no you don't," I growled, giving the reins a sharp pull and digging my heels into her ribs. She collected herself neatly and moved into a smooth-as-silk lope. Chalk up one round to me.

I tried a couple of figure eights and was amazed at how light on the bit she was. For a beat-up, sour old horse, she reined like she had power steering. I could have loped around there for half the night, but I didn't dare risk damaging her bad leg. I took her back to the corral and jumped off. Cole was waiting.

"Did you see the way she reined?" I asked, patting her neck and then giving the itchy spots under the cheek pieces of the bridle a rub. "She's got the most beautiful lope." I caught myself babbling—and to Cole McCall of all people. But horses sometimes do that to me. I get carried away.

Cole shrugged, unimpressed. "Yeah, could be worse." Then he gave her a long, thoughtful look. "So, you got her named yet?"

I shook my head. In the time I'd known this horse, most of the names that had crossed my mind weren't fit to say out loud.

"Well, blue roans are pretty rare. Maybe you should just call her Blue."

I gave him a pained look. "That sounds like some old hound dog in a country song."

"There something wrong with country music?"

I just rolled my eyes. "She's got a neat white mark like a crescent moon on her forehead. Maybe I should call her Crescent."

"Crescent isn't a horse. It's a wrench."

"Okay, then how about just Moon?"

Cole burst right out laughing at that. "The last thing Moon makes me think of is a mark on a horse's face."

"Well, what you think doesn't matter a whole lot. She's my horse."

Cole gave me his most irritating grin. "Except for seven bucks worth of her."

"I'll trim her hoofs and give you the trimmings. How's that?"

He laughed and then ran his hand along the swollen place on her leg. "You know, this swelling would go down faster if you'd pack it in ice for a while."

"Sure, Cole. Learn that in veterinary school?"

He shrugged. "Suit yourself. I gotta go."

As soon as he was out of sight, I went in and got the ice.

Chapter Eight

The ice really did seem to help, so I repeated it every night for a week. Finally, the roan wasn't limping at all and the swelling was almost gone. Her ribs didn't stick out so much as her sides rounded out under the shiny gray-blue hide. Meanwhile, I was riding her, finding out more about her. She was starting to trust me and I was beginning to see the real horse behind the scarecrow I'd bought at the auction. There was nothing more I could teach her about reining or taking the right leads. She just naturally did it right. Somebody, somewhere, had put a lot of training into her. I couldn't help wondering who, where—and how come I got lucky enough to pick her up so cheap. But I wasn't so sure I really wanted to know.

Anyway, she was ready to start learning about barrel racing. I collected three old, dented-up barrels from the shed and set them up in a triangle. Then I started practicing the cloverleaf pattern around them. I could see that this was something the mare hadn't done before, but she caught on fast. After a couple of days of taking her through the pattern at a trot, I started letting her go a little. She was fast as greased lightning between the turns. She went around the barrels close as a dust rag going around a table leg. So close, in fact, that it wasn't long before I had developed permanent dents in my shinbones.

After a few good whacks I started wearing an old sweatshirt wrapped around each knee. Cole almost killed himself laughing the first time he saw my new outfit, but I didn't care. They weren't his shins.

Another couple of weeks passed, one day sliding into another. Help Dad all day. Work with my mare in the evening. It seemed like it was going to go on that way all summer.

It was only about seven-fifteen one morning when I heard the unmistakable sound of Cole's truck rumbling into the yard. I wondered what had moved him to show up so early, but since I was washing my hair in the shower at that moment, I couldn't ask him. I did manage to get dried and dressed in something under two minutes, though.

I arrived in the yard to find my whole family lined up like some sort of a welcoming committee. Dad and Cole were off to the side, talking. When Dad saw me he called me over. "Bobbie Jo, Cole's dad would like to see your new horse," he said.

I stared at him. So? I thought. Why does this require some kind of grand performance? Why doesn't he just haul himself out of that truck and walk twenty steps to the corral and have a look?

I guess Dad could read my thoughts. Before I could blurt out something rude or stupid he said, "Go and bring her over here, Bobbie Jo." He gave me his "and don't argue" look.

I shrugged and went to catch the horse. When I got back, the passenger door of the truck was open and Dad and Cole were both standing beside it. It looked like they were lifting something out. They were. It was a man. The man finally got both feet on the ground—sort of—but mainly stood balancing himself on a pair of crutches. On the crutches and on two twisted legs that seemed ready to buckle beneath him. I managed to drag my stare away from the legs long enough to look at the man's face. It matched the legs just fine. Gaunt and hard and set in lines of permanent pain. It was the face of a man who had been to hell and hadn't made it all the way back yet.

I caught myself staring, so I focused my eyes on a fascinating clump of grass beside my foot.

Cole cleared his throat. "Mr. and Mrs. Brooks, Bobbie Jo, Sara, this is my dad, Jim McCall." The words came out low and kind of scratchy, as if they hurt his throat. Mom and Dad managed to babble something polite. Sara just stared, for once at a loss for words. I think I said hi.

The man just nodded, like talking was something he'd left behind a long time ago. He didn't seem interested in us anyway. His eyes, bright blue like Cole's, were the only part of him, that seemed alive. They were fixed on my blue roan mare. Leaning heavily on the crutches, he took a staggering step toward her. Dad started to reach out a hand to help him, but Cole shook his head. Dad pulled back his hand and McCall fought his way over to the mare on his own. I tightened my grip on the halter rope. This horse had come a long way, but she still could be jumpy. It would be just like her to spook seven ways to sundown at the sight of this man with four legs—two of which were big sticks.

Then Jim McCall spoke to her. I didn't even really catch the words. Just the usual stuff you say to a horse. But the words didn't matter. He had the gentlest voice I'd ever heard. Peaceful. Kind of like a lazy river flowing around a bend under a warm summer sun. Right away I knew it hit the horse the same way. Her ears flickered with interest, and I could feel the tension flow right out of her.

Next thing I knew, McCall was leaning against her shoulder. He ran his hand along her hard-muscled neck, and she was loving every minute of it. I didn't know where this guy had come from or how he'd got so messed up, but one thing was for sure. With horses he was a natural. Slowly, he worked his way around my horse, sizing her up from every angle. He kept right on talking to her and ignoring the rest of us like he and the horse were on a desert island somewhere. He paused a long time studying the shoulder with the wagon wheel brand. He gently ran his hand back and forth over it, without a word to anyone.

Then he even convinced her to open her mouth and had a careful look at her teeth. At last he gave my horse one final pat on the neck and made his way back to the truck. Cole helped him in and I thought he was going to leave the way he came, without a word to any of us. But he focused those piercing eyes on me through the truck's open window. "Look after that horse, Bobbie Jo," he said, real soft like he'd talked to the mare. "One like that only comes along once in a blue moon." He nodded to Cole and they drove away.

As the truck rumbled off down the lane, Sara blurted out what must have nearly killed her to keep to herself that long. "That's Cole's father? I thought it was his grandfather."

Nobody bothered to answer her. We all walked to the house, thinking and wondering. I wasn't sure what was going through everybody else's mind, but mine kept repeating the only words Jim McCall had spoken to me. There was something real important in those words. And suddenly I knew what it was. He had just named my horse. Blue Moon.

Chapter Nine

The summer kept rolling by. Haying started. The work was long and hard and hot. Cole showed up the same time every morning, but he never brought his dad again. Cole never even mentioned him. Some unwritten law kept us from mentioning him either.

Evenings were still riding time. I was turning Blue Moon into a barrel horse. I'd carefully measured out the distance between my barrels so they were pretty well the same as for most outdoor arenas. Blue Moon kept running the pattern in under eighteen seconds. Another few days and I was going to look for a rodeo to enter.

That was the plan. But Blue Moon had other plans. It was a hot, muggy evening. We'd been hauling hay as fast as we could all day because Dad expected rain. Now I was ready for today's first run around the barrels. Blue Moon was dancing, keyed up, tossing her head with excitement. I nodded to Cole, who was holding the stopwatch. When I loosened the reins, Blue Moon shot forward like a rocket. Around the first barrel, digging for traction in the loose dirt, then running hard for the second. Around it so tight I could almost hear my shinbone crying out for mercy. Then the long run to the third barrel. Around it and the flat-out race across the finish line. I rode her around in a big circle to slow her down and then to a sliding stop almost toe-to-toe with Cole's scuffed old boots.

"Well?" I asked breathlessly. I always forget to breathe when I'm barrel racing and end up more winded than the horse.

He looked up from the watch. "Well what?" he asked with an irritating grin. Before I could let him have it with the end of my reins, his memory returned. "Seventeen-two," he said.

I gave a whoop that startled Blue Moon so bad she almost jumped out from under me. "Seventeen-two! That's four-tenths faster than she's ever gone. One more time. We're gonna break seventeen this time."

Cole just shrugged. "Maybe," he said. "Maybe you should quit while you're still ahead." But I was already loping away to line up for another run. It was even faster. I could feel it. Not a fraction of a second lost anywhere. No slips. No wasted steps. We were coming up on the final barrel, the one closest to the barn. Now, one lightning turn around it and...

The mare didn't turn. I was giving her the signal with the reins, with my knees, with my whole body, but she wasn't turning. Instead, she had the bit in her teeth and was pounding straight for the barn, faster than she'd ever run before. I gave up trying to turn her. I just wanted to stop her. But there was no way. I might as well have been trying to stop a locomotive. She was heading straight for the open barn door, and I knew she wasn't planning to stop. There was only one problem. The doorway was high enough for a horse. But not for a horse with a rider on its back. If I didn't do something fast, I was about to lose my head.

I jerked my feet out of the stirrups and took a quick glance at the green blur beneath Blue Moon's pounding hoofs. I took a deep breath and bailed off. Hitting the ground knocked that breath right back out of me.

I was just considering trying to move when strong arms suddenly went around me. "Bobbie Jo, are you all right? Don't try to move." I immediately sat up—and found myself looking into Cole's eyes. It was the first time I'd seen them at such close range.

They were real worried-looking. They were also the most beautiful eyes I'd ever seen on anybody.

I groaned. I must have hit my head. Nothing short of brain damage would get me thinking like that.

"Are you sure you're okay?"

"Of course I'm okay," I said grumpily. I staggered to my feet, swayed a little and felt Cole reach out to steady me. His arms around me felt so good that for a minute I just stood there letting him hold me.

Then I broke away. "What got into that crazy horse anyway?"

"She went sour."

"What?"

"How many times you figure you've run those barrels with her in the last couple of weeks?"

I thought a minute. "Sixty maybe?"

Cole nodded. "At least. She's had enough of it. She's bored and she's mad and I think she just made her point. She needs a change."

I started to open my mouth to argue and then shut it again. I couldn't think of any arguments. Everything Cole had said made sense. Just because she'd been learning so fast was no excuse for me to push her so hard. I gave Cole a dirty look for being right and went into the barn to get her.

Blue Moon was standing in her stall, ladylike as could be, munching on some hay. "Sorry, girl," I whispered into a black-tipped ear. "I get the message. But next time, could you explain a little more gently?"

I led her outside and climbed stiffly back into the saddle. "I'm gonna ride her down to the river. Give her a change of scenery." I nodded toward the corral where Patchy Pete was standing. "You can borrow Patchy if you want to come along."

Cole laughed. "I'll pass. I hate it when my feet drag on the ground when I'm riding. See you later, Blue Jeans."

I sat watching as he jumped into his truck and rumbled down the lane. I breathed a sigh of relief. At last, some riding time without

Cole hanging around. And then I caught myself missing him. Maybe I really had hit my head.

I let the mare take her time as I rode along the wide grassy ditch at the edge of the road. The ride to the river should take about an hour. Just time enough to get there and back before dark.

I was deep in a daydream, and I think Blue Moon was too. Suddenly, the sound of hoofbeats woke us both up. Blue Moon shot a look over her shoulder and whinnied. I looked over my shoulder, too. A rider was coming up behind us at a lope. He was on a powerfully built black horse and he was gaining fast. I stared for a few long seconds until I saw that the rider was Cole McCall.

Where had that horse come from? Suddenly, I realized just how little I really knew about the McCalls. Living back there in the trees at the end of that long lane, they could have a dozen horses for all I knew.

Cole pulled the big horse down to a walk and came up beside us. "Hi, Blue Jeans," he said with a grin. "Imagine runnin' into you out here."

I ignored him and studied the horse. A stallion, nearly sixteen hands tall. He had the deep-muscled shoulders and hindquarters of a purebred quarter horse. He was jet-black except for a white star on his forehead. "Where did you get that horse?" I demanded.

"Stole him off a dead gunfighter," Cole drawled.

I glared at him. "Cole..."

"Raised him from a colt," he said, and this time I could see he meant it.

I stared at him unbelievingly. "All this time you've been watching me work with Blue Moon you never once said anything about having a horse of your own. Why didn't you tell me?"

Cole shrugged, reached down and rubbed the stallion's neck. "Itchy, huh, Nightstar?" Then he looked up. "Did you ever ask?" he said, his eyes on mine.

Before I had time to answer, Nightstar reached his nose over toward Blue Moon and gave a soft little whinny. It sounded like it meant something like, "How about we ditch these two and go eat clover together in the moonlight?"

Blue Moon gave an insulted squeal, flattened her ears and bared her teeth. I grinned and gave her a pat on the neck. She was definitely my kind of horse.

Chapter Ten

Cole and I started riding together nearly every evening. The longer rides were just what Blue Moon needed. When I tried her on the barrels again, she was back to behaving like a pro. Now what she needed was a chance to prove herself. I guess Cole was thinking the same thing. One Monday morning he handed me a piece of paper. It was a poster for the Elkridge Rodeo. He pointed to an event near the bottom of the page. Novice Barrel Racing. "No pros in there," he said. "Ol' Moonface would have a pretty good chance."

I jabbed him in the ribs with my elbow. "Stop calling her that!" Then I couldn't resist adding, "You really think she could win?"

"Sure," he said with a wicked grin, "if she doesn't decide to skip the third barrel and run for home instead."

I gave him another jab. "Not much danger," I said confidently. Especially since home was a two-hour drive from Elkridge. I started to work on Dad. I had two weeks to talk him into the three things I needed. His truck. His trailer. And his permission to go. By the end of the week I had all three.

That was about the same time that Cole started acting funny. I mean even stranger than usual. I'd be yapping away at him about Blue Moon, and he'd get this worried look on his face and say something like, "Uh, Bobbie Jo, there's something I'd better..."

Bobbie Jo yet, not Blue Jeans. But when I'd stop talking and wait to hear what he had to say, he'd never get around to spitting it out. It was really getting on my nerves.

The day before the rodeo, I was bouncing off the ground with excitement. Cole was grumpy as an old bear with a hangover.

I took Blue Moon for just one quick run around the barrels that evening. She did them in seventeen-one. "Cole!" I screeched when he told me. "That's fantastic! She's gonna win!"

"Yeah," he said, staring at the ground. "Maybe."

I couldn't take it. "Well thanks a lot for the support. All week you've been trying to bring me down and I've had enough of it. Just go home."

I thought at least he'd fight back. He didn't. He just nodded. "Okay. Good luck tomorrow."

It felt like I slept about ten minutes that night. In the morning I woke up tired and scared. I didn't want to go to the rodeo alone.

Everything I'd done with Blue Moon, I'd done by myself. I kept telling myself that. It was the truth. But every step of the way, Cole had been there. Not doing all that much. Just being there. And suddenly I realized I still needed him to be there.

I spent the morning going through the motions of getting ready to go to the rodeo. It was Saturday, so Cole didn't come to work. He didn't come to hang around either, like he did most Saturdays.

It was almost one o'clock. I should get going. I wanted to watch some of the other events and give Blue Moon lots of time to get used to the place. I put the mare in the trailer. Cole and I had been practicing loading her for weeks. Now she walked right in. I didn't have any excuse to hang around any longer.

Mom and Dad came out to wish me luck. They had wanted to come and watch me race, but one of our best cows was due to calve that day so they didn't dare leave. As I climbed into the truck, Mom asked the question I'd been dreading. "Isn't Cole going with you, Bobbie Jo? After all the time he's spent helping you with the horse, I thought you'd want him to be there for your first rodeo."

I swallowed hard, blinked and avoided my mother's eyes. "I don't need Cole McCall holding my hand every move I make." Then I rammed the truck into gear and took off with a jolt that probably spoiled Blue Moon's day.

All the way down the lane I could still see my parents in the rearview mirror staring after me. I would have bet they were shaking their heads.

I turned onto the main road, wiping a hand across my eyes and wondering why the windshield was so blurry. I drove slowly past Cole's turnoff, staring as far as I could see down the empty lane. Suddenly, I hit the brakes. "Sorry again, Blue Moon," I muttered as the truck jolted to a stop. I backed up and turned into the lane. I wasn't sure what I was doing, but I couldn't stop myself.

Not until I was halfway around the curve. Then I stopped real sudden. If I hadn't, I would have run head-on into Cole's truck coming from the opposite direction. He hit the brakes, too. Then he pulled his truck off to the side, came running over and jumped in beside me. "Cole..." I began, but I didn't know what to say. It didn't matter because he interrupted me anyway.

"Hey, Blue Jeans," he said with that teasing grin. "You weren't gonna go without me, were you?"

I spent the next twenty minutes trying to back the trailer around the curve. Cole spent the next twenty minutes laughing at me trying to back the trailer around the curve. Things were back to normal—for now anyway.

The afternoon that had stretched out ahead was suddenly gone. The afternoon rodeo events ended and everything shut down for an hour. Time to warm up the barrel horses. Blue Moon was calm, in control. She took the crowds and confusion in her stride. Somewhere, in a past life, Blue Moon had definitely been around.

The barrel racing started. The first rider was slow as molasses. Nineteen-five. We could beat that. The next two riders knocked down barrels. Five-second penalties. Out of luck. Then a girl came out on a beautiful golden palomino that ran like the wind. She ran clean—seventeen-six. My stomach knotted. Then came a real young kid on a big bay. She was just going into the first turn when a sudden gust of wind came up. The wind whirled a big piece of cardboard out of the stands and almost into her horse's face. He leaped straight sideways, slammed her leg against the barrel, lost his footing and fell. They took the girl out in an ambulance. The horse limped out bleeding from a big cut on his leg.

It was a hot summer evening but I felt myself go cold inside. Did I really know what to expect from my horse? And why did I have to draw second-last place in the running order? Just one left before me. A young horse. Green as grass at this business. but the rider was experienced. She steered the horse around the barrels and turned for home. That's when he ducked his head and went to bucking. The girl stayed with him and rode out the storm. The crowd loved it. Except for me, that is. All I felt was a little closer to throwing up.

Then I heard my name over the PA system. I went on autopilot. Somehow I got Blue Moon lined up behind the starting line. I felt the pent-up power underneath me. She was ready. I gulped a deep breath, looked up and caught a glimpse of Cole giving me the thumbs-up signal from the fence. Then we were gone. How could so few seconds stretch out so long? I felt each powerful stride as Blue Moon closed in on the first barrel, dug in and turned on a dime. I felt her powerful hindquarters push her away from that barrel and on toward the second one. Close around. Pounding down the long stretch to barrel three. Around it and racing for home.

Then I was circling her to a stop and waiting, breathless as always, for the time. It boomed out from the announcer's stand. "We have a new leader, folks. B.J. Brooks and Blue Moon, seventeen-three."

The grandstand went wild with cheering. I reached down and hugged Blue Moon's neck. She gave her head a casual toss. "No big deal," I think she said. But when we'd moved out of the arena, Cole came up and gave her a hug, too. If you really want to know, Blue Moon wasn't the only one he hugged. And, yes, I did hug him back.

The last horse ran eighteen flat. Blue Moon and I loped out of the arena with our first trophy just as it started to rain.

Chapter Eleven

The rain stayed with us as darkness fell and we drove into the night. The main highway was busy with a lot of big trucks throwing water up over my windshield. I was relieved when we turned off onto the two-lane highway for the last halfhour of the drive. Then the storm really hit. The sky just opened up and the rain was a solid sheet in front of us. The noise on the truck's roof was enough to rattle my brains. I hoped that Blue Moon wasn't too scared back there.

I slowed down to a crawl, stared hard through the curtain of water and tried to keep track of the white line on the highway. We started into a long, gentle curve—and suddenly everything happened at once. A pair of headlights cut through the rain almost straight ahead of me. Cole yelled, "Look out!" and I swung the wheel to the right.

A bunch of miracles happened in the next split second. The other driver managed to swerve back into his own lane. I managed to stop my swerve before I rolled both the truck and the trailer. We skidded to a stop with just one front truck wheel in the shallow ditch.

The minute we stopped moving I was piling out the door. I slid my way along the rain-slick highway to the trailer and yanked open the small door at the side. Blue Moon was on her feet, standing kind of straddled out like a person on the deck of a rocking boat. I reached in and rubbed her neck. "It's okay, Moon. It's gonna be all right." She gave a nervous little whinny and reached over to take a nip out of the sleeve of my jacket. I think she was making a statement about my driving. I gave her another pat and then gently closed the door.

"Thank God she's okay," I said over my shoulder to Cole. There was no answer. I turned around to face him, but he wasn't there. I was sure he'd have been out of the truck in a flash and right behind me to check on the horse.

I went back to the open driver's side door. Cole hadn't moved. He was sitting with both hands gripping the edge of the dashboard, staring straight ahead. "Cole? Are you hurt? Did you hit your head or something?" I started to panic. "Cole! Talk to me!"

He sort of shook his head and relaxed his death grip on the dash. "Sorry, Bobbie Jo," he said in a voice that was almost a whisper. "For a minute there I thought it was all happening again."

I laid my hand on his shoulder. "What, Cole?" I asked softly. "What was happening again?"

He took a deep breath. "Is the horse okay?" he asked. I nodded. "Are we stuck?"

"I think if I put it in four-wheel drive we can get out. Just one wheel went in."

"Okay, let's go home. I'll tell you on the way."

He told me. It was a long story. "We used to live in Texas. My dad was head trainer for one of the biggest quarter horse ranches in the country. We were building up a herd of our own, too. We'd just put down a payment on a place of our own. Then," his voice went kind of shaky, "one night we were comin' home from the city in a thunderstorm and a drunk driver hit our truck. We all got hurt." He turned and lifted up the side of his shoulder-length hair to show me the angry red scar on his neck. "A piece of pipe we were hauling came through the back window and got me. Mom had a broken arm. But Dad...." His voice broke. He swallowed. "You've seen Dad. He couldn't work anymore. We didn't have medical insurance. The doctor bills took everything. We saved Nightstar and two mares. That's all. This is my uncle's place we're living on here. He's owned the land for a long time, but he lives in Calgary. He said we'd at least have a roof over our heads." He gave me a shaky smile.

"Dad goes to the hospital for therapy every day now. It's been a year and a half since the accident, but this is the first he's been willing to even try. At first he just wanted to die. But he's startin' to care a little now. Comin' to see Blue Moon was the first time he's gone out amongst people since we got here. I guess I'd talked about her so much his curiosity finally got the best of him." Cole grinned. "He sure took to that horse. Talked about her more than he's talked about anything since the accident."

Suddenly, the smile faded and I knew something else was wrong. "Tell me the rest, Cole," I said, glancing at his face in the glow of the instrument panel.

He wouldn't look at me. "That's all there is to tell about my family," he said in a low voice.

"But there's something else you've got to tell me, isn't there? You've been trying to get up the nerve to tell me all week, Cole. Get it over with." I turned the corner into our lane and pulled to a stop in front of the barn. In a minute, my family would be out here wanting to know how everything went. I wanted an answer first.

Cole slowly reached into the front pocket of his jean jacket and brought out a folded piece of paper. I opened it and turned on the overhead light.

It was a poster.

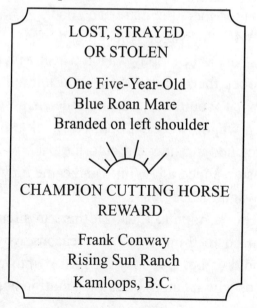

LOST, STRAYED
OR STOLEN

One Five-Year-Old
Blue Roan Mare
Branded on left shoulder

CHAMPION CUTTING HORSE
REWARD

Frank Conway
Rising Sun Ranch
Kamloops, B.C.

I sat there staring at the paper. Then I stared at Cole. "Where...?" I began. "How...?" There were so many questions I didn't know where to start.

Cole answered some of them. "Like I said, Dad couldn't get the mare off his mind. He kept saying she reminded him of something. Finally he got out a bunch of papers and dug through them. The poster was put out by a friend of his in Kamloops. He sent Dad a copy just in case he ever ran across a clue to where the mare had gone."

"But the wagon wheel brand..."

"Yeah, the sloppy wagon wheel with the spokes that don't line up. You know how easy it would be to change the rising sun to a wagon wheel? Look." He took a pen, sketched a rising sun onto the back of the poster, added a few lines and came up with a wagon wheel.

For a minute, I just sat there in silence. I tried to think of all the reasons why it couldn't be. But they all turned into reasons why it could. Champion cutting horse.

I remembered that first morning when Dad had found Blue Moon out there rounding up cows all by herself.

"Dad says it's up to you what you do about the horse. He's not gonna do anything. He just figured you had a right to know, that's all."

Before I could answer there was a loud tap on the window. I opened the door. There stood Sara. "You guys steamin' up the windows in there or what?" she asked with a sly grin.

"Get lost, rodent," I said. I would have said more, but Mom and Dad were right behind her. They spotted the trophy and got all excited and proud the way parents are supposed to. I did my best to act excited and proud, too. But it was all I could do to keep it together long enough to look after Blue Moon and drive Cole home. Then I shut myself in my room and cried myself to sleep.

But I didn't stay asleep. I kept waking up and asking myself what I was going to do. Blue Moon was mine, wasn't she? After all, if I hadn't bought her, she'd be dead by

103

now. But what if I'd been the one she'd been stolen from? What if somebody had her and knew she belonged to me but wouldn't even let me know she was still alive?

First thing in the morning, I phoned Frank Conway in Kamloops. I think I got the guy out of bed. I forgot that it was an hour earlier in B.C.

I told him the whole story. It took a while. Not only was I going to lose my horse, I'd be broke for a year paying off this phone call. At first, Conway wasn't convinced. But the more I told him, the more I could sense he was listening.

He asked directions to our place. He had business in Alberta the next week, he said. He'd come by and have a look at her. "Okay, that'll be fine," I said. Then I hung up the phone and bawled some more.

The week dragged by. Half the time I practically lived in the corral, not wanting to miss a single minute of the time I had left with Blue Moon. Then I'd get tough and stay away from her for a whole day, practicing for when she wouldn't be there. I finally told Mom and Dad what was happening. They were real proud that I'd done the right thing. My dad gave me lots of neat little speeches on building character and stuff. Personally, I'd rather have the horse than the character. Even Sara started being nice to me, so I guess I must have been in pretty bad shape.

Friday afternoon, Cole and I were stacking square bales in the hay shed. He suddenly straightened up and stood looking down the lane. "Bobbie Jo," he said softly. I followed the direction of his gaze and saw a gray half-ton with B.C. plates pulling into the yard. Cole gave me a long look. "You okay?" he asked. I nodded. He put his arm around my shoulders and we went to meet Frank Conway. When we got closer I realized Conway wasn't alone. Jim McCall was in the passenger seat. He stayed in the truck as Conway got out and introduced himself.

I managed a "hello" and then turned away fast to go and get the horse. I'd been all set to hate Mr. Conway. It was kind of a disappointment when I couldn't. But as soon as I saw the way he handled the mare, I knew the guy was okay. He talked to her real quiet, ran a firm but gentle hand down her shoulder and walked all around her, looking her over. He studied the brand for a long time and then shook his head. He checked her legs and her hoofs. He was just trying to get her to open her mouth to check her teeth when the truck door closed behind us. We all turned around in time to see Cole's dad walking toward us. He still had the crutches but his legs were straighter and he was putting weight on them. "Never mind the teeth, Frank," he said with something close to a grin. "I checked them. The age works out right."

There was a silence. Conway cleared his throat. He pushed aside her forelock. "Well, then, it's her. The brand, the age, but mostly this funny little mark on her face." He reached into his pocket and brought out a picture of a blue roan colt. Beneath its short, fuzzy forelock was a perfect crescent moon. He laid a hand on her neck. "Her name's Bonnie Blue, and you'll never know how much it means to me to find her."

Uh-uh, I thought to myself, her name's Blue Moon, and you'll never know how much it means to me to lose her.

"So, how much did you say you paid for her, Bobbie Jo?" Conway asked.

I told him. Yeah, I thought. If I get real lucky you might give me back my $690.00—and you get the greatest horse in the world.

Just then, Jim McCall spoke up. "Come over here a minute, Frank. Let's see if you're half the horse trader you used to be."

Conway laughed and walked over to where Cole's dad was leaning on the fence. They talked, low-voiced, for a while. Quite a while. I saw Conway shake his head a couple of times. He looked in Blue Moon's direction a few times. Finally, he nodded and came back to where Blue Moon was standing.

"Jim tells me you beat a meat buyer out of this mare at an auction sale. That true, Bobbie Jo?" I nodded, wondering where this conversation was going. "In some countries they believe if you save someone's life, you're responsible for them forever," he said. Now I really wondered where this conversation was going. "And," he went on, "you couldn't very well be responsible for a horse that was way off in B.C., could you?"

I just kind of gawked at him. He turned to Cole. "When I stopped by your place, your dad showed me your black stallion. Some kind of a horse, isn't he?"

"Yes, sir," Cole agreed, his voice cautious. I could see he was wondering what was going on here, too.

"Your dad figures that if Bonnie Blue here was bred to your black, she might just come up with a pretty special kind of colt." Conway turned back to look at me. "So, here's the deal, Bobbie Jo. You let this mare raise me a foal from Cole's stallion and I'll consider it full payment for the mare. Sound fair to you?"

For once in my life I was stuck for words. I just stood there nodding my head so hard I thought I could hear my brains rattle. Frank Conway held out his hand. "Deal," he said.

"Deal," I said. We shook on it.

Cole grinned. "Blue Jeans and Blue Moon. Great name for a country music act."

I swatted him. But not too hard.

NEW
Orca Soundings novel

Overdrive by Eric Walters

"Go! Get out of here!"
I saw flashing red lights behind me in the distance. For a split second I took my foot off the accelerator. Then I pressed down harder and took a quick left turn.

Jake has finally got his driver's license, and tonight he has his brother's car as well. He and his friend Mickey take the car out and cruise the strip. When they challenge another driver to a road race, a disastrous chain reaction causes an accident. Jake and Mickey leave the scene, trying to convince themselves they were not involved. The driver of the other car was Luke, a one-time friend of Jakes. Jake finds he cannot pretend it didn't happen and struggles with the right thing to do. Should he pretend he was not involved and hope Luke doesn't remember? Or should he go to the police?